MW00779229

DUCKS OF THE MISSISSIPPI

FLYWAY

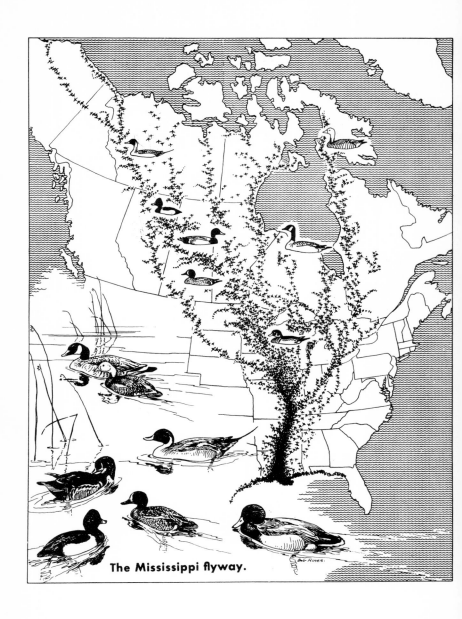

The Mississippi flyway.

DUCKS of the
Mississippi Flyway

Illustrated by Ken Haag and Ernest Strubbe

Text by John McKane

NORTH STAR PRESS
ST. CLOUD, MINNESOTA

© Copyright 1969
by
Ken Haag
ALL RIGHTS RESERVED
Library of Congress Catalog Number 79-105937
Printed in the United States of America

FOREWORD TO THE FIRST EDITION

Finding inspiration in waterfowl is an ageless quest that has begirt man since earliest times. Whether caught by the vivid plumages of ducks or their free spirited flight, we have always identified with them.

Ancient Egyptian paintings suggest our fascination for ducks is not merely of spirit. Through the ages man has delighted in them for table feasts unequaled — that of a roast bird.

These gay clad, feathered creatures recur in the folklore, art, literature, mythology, and heritages of the world. Certain American Indian tribes dance a duck dance. From trout flies to pillow down, ducks have given us varied, inherent qualities.

In featuring ducks of the 'Mississippi Flyway' we do point to particular significance of vast areas of breeding territory therein attributed, with Minnesota the 'watermost' state in the flyway.

In olden days many Minnesota lakes and marshes were renowned for waterfowling. Some still are. Most famous of all was Heron Lake, a large shallow prairie basin in Jackson county. Hunters from as far as Dublin, Ireland hunted there before the turn of the century. Heron Lake is again propagating waterfowl thanks to the efforts of farmers of the North Heron Lake Game Producers Association.

Many other lakes in Minnesota hold fortunes for hunter and birder alike. Frog Lake in Stevens County (which is background for many of the illustrations in this book) is a prime Redhead, Ruddy nesting lake in North America.

With strong emphasis on nesting areas in Minnesota our illustrations show ducks in breeding plumage. Annual production of ducks in Minnesota is estimated to close to a million birds. These birds likely provide up to one fourth of the take by Minnesota hunters. Hunters in Minnesota usually harvest more ducks than any of the other 13 states of the Mississippi Flyway.

Knowing the kinds of ducks we have in Minnesota is essential in understanding the need for prairie potholes, wooded streams, and other nesting habitat.

With thirty-one species of ducks recorded in Minnesota, twenty being common migrants, the need is great; for realizing our rich heritage, conserving our habitat, knowing the ducks, and finally plying our resources to this end — as the philosopher Montaigne wrote: "Why may not a waterfowl say thus: 'All the parts of the universe I have an interest in; the earth serves me to walk upon, the sun to light me; the stars have guiding influence upon me; I have advantage by the winds and such by the waters; there is nothing that yon heavenly room looks upon so favorably as me. I am the darling of Nature: It is not man that keeps, lodges, and serves me?' "

To this we add; and sustains me.

— Ken Haag

Two of the thirty-one species of ducks found in the Mississippi Flyway are not pictured in this series. They are the Common Scoter and King Eider, neither of which are regular migrants through Minnesota.

COMMON SCOTER — In North America this blackish relative of the White Winged Scoter breeds primarily on the coast of Alaska. It winters along both the Atlantic and Pacific coasts. The male has a prominent orange-yellow protuberance at the base of the upper bill. The female is lighter in color and shows grayish color on the sides of the face. When this species does occur in the state it usually is found on Lake Superior during the winter months.

KING EIDER — This duck of the far north has been recorded only twice in the state of Minnesota, both times on Lake Superior during the winter. King Eiders nest in the tundra near the Arctic coasts of Canada, Alaska, Greenland, Siberia, and Russia. Though they winter exclusively at sea, usually in the region of the Aleutians, Pacific, and Gulf of St. Lawrence on the Atlantic, some apparently find the Great Lakes area on occasion.

PREFACE

"Waterfowl of the Mississippi Flyway" is more than a mere guide, reference or collector's item. It is designed to bring together, in authentic, beautiful, full-color reproductions, that segment of our North American waterfowl family which is the priceless heritage of all who reside along this great Flyway.

In Ken Haag's inspiring paintings of 22 species, and in the eight selected works of Ernest Strubbe, both native Minnesota artists, we have captured the majesty of our waterfowl in full spring plumage.

Of what value are waterfowl? What measure of worth does one assign to the splash of color in autumn leaves, the beauty of a sunset, or the haunting solitude of a great forest? Such values transcend mercenary considerations, for they belong to all generations for all time.

We are indebted to the Minnesota Conservation Department on two counts: For the classic *"Save the Wetlands"* program initiated in 1951, a fundamental concept of habitat preservation which, thankfully, is now international in scope, and for the superb references which were most helpful in compiling this publication.

We dedicate this work to all who treasure our waterfowl, whether they be casual observers, hunters, bird-watchers, or youngsters still too young in years to have an awareness of the urgency of that ceaseless conservation struggle to perpetuate our outdoor heritage.

—John G. McKane

DABBLERS   DIVERS

Dabblers are most characteristic of small bodies of water. When taking flight, they spring directly into the air; they obtain food by dabbling or tipping up rather than by diving. *Divers* are ducks of more open bodies of water, although they breed on marshes. They dive for their food, and take flight by pattering along the water while getting underway.

INDEX TO DUCKS

Duck	page
Mallard	2
Black Duck	4
Pintail	6
Green Winged Teal	8
Blue Winged Teal	10
Cinnamon Teal and Shoveller	12
Gadwall	14
European Widgeon and Baldpate	16
Wood Duck	18
Canvasback	20
Redhead	22
Ring-necked Duck	24
Lesser Scaup	26
Greater Scaup	28
Ruddy Duck	30
Bufflehead	32
Common Goldeneye	34
Barrows Goldeneye	36
Old Squaw	38
Harlequin	40
Red Breasted Merganser	42
American Merganser	44
Hooded Merganser	46
White Winged Scoter and Common Eider	48
Surf Scoter	50
Fulvous Tree Duck	52
American Coot	54
Topography of a Duck	56

MALLARD
(Anas platyrhynchos platyrhynchos)

Other Common Names
Greenhead (males), Gray Duck (females)

Field Notes
This bird is recognized as the "King of Sport Ducks" throughout the United States and Canada. The Mallard is valued not only by the hunter, but as a table delicacy as well. Wary by nature, the Mallard is strong of flight and not easily fooled by decoys "the second time around." On occasion, the harvest of Mallards on the Mississippi Flyway has exceeded that of all other ducks.

Mallards congregate in large marshes the first part of October and are present until the first week in November, or until the first general freeze-up. This is the time of the "northern flight" or the "Grand Passage."

Field Marks
Prefers wooded swamps and marshes. Average weights in fall range from 2 pounds 8 ounces for immature ducks to 3 pounds for adult males. *Male*: Know him by that green head and narrow white neck band, ruddy breast and white tail. *Female*: Mottled brown with prominent white borders on each side of metallic-blue wing patch, and whitish tail.

Range
Breeds throughout the Upper Midwest, and from Alaska to western New York and northern California. The Mallard is one of earliest ducks to migrate north in the spring. This versatile bird will range as far north into Canada as open water and food supplies permit. Winters from Great Lakes and southern New England to the Gulf of Mexico.

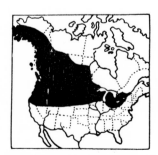

Principal breeding ranges of the Mallard in Minnesota and in North America.

Mallard

♀

♂

BLACK DUCK
(Anas rubripes)

Other Common Names
Black Mallard

Field Notes
Since Minnesota marks the most westerly portion of the Black Duck's range in the United States, this duck makes up less than one per cent of the annual bag in the North Star State. It is, however, the most abundant bird available to eastern hunters and is ranked with the Mallard as a desirable game species there.

Often associated with lakes and marshes in woodland habitat, the Black Duck, while preferring to nest on the ground in vegetation near marsh edges, has been known to use the old nests of other birds — in trees!

Field Marks
As the name suggests, this duck has dark plumage. When at rest, the general appearance of both sexes is blackish. In flights, the bird's dark color and flashing white wing linings are the telltale identifying features. The neck and head are somewhat lighter in color than the body. Color of the bill ranges from greenish-yellow to yellow and the feet from pink to red. Size is slightly larger than Mallard.

Range
While the Black Duck's range extends into northeastern Minnesota, Wisconsin and northern Illinois, this is primarily a duck of eastern North America. Primary breeding ground in Minnesota is in the forested northeastern counties. The principal wintering areas are on the Atlantic coast from New England to North Carolina.

Principal breeding ranges of the Black Duck in Minnesota and North America.

4

Black Duck ♀

♂

PINTAIL
(Anas acuta acuta)

Other Common Names
Sprig, Sprig-tail

Field Notes
"Alert" is the word for this comparatively large, slender and graceful bird. Due to its early fall migration, it comprises a small portion of the hunter's bag in Minnesota, and about five per cent of the total harvest along the Mississippi Flyway. But its size and excellent table qualities make it a prized specimen.

The Pintail commonly frequents small marshes and marshy edges of lakes where it feeds by tipping-up. But Pintails are also fond of insects, particularly grasshoppers, and swathed grain and rice. Prefers dry land for nesting. Average weight is 2 pounds 2 ounces and for females, 1 pound 13 ounces.

Field Marks
The Pintail can be distinguished by its slim outline, pointed wings and that long, pointed "pin" tail. *Male*: Prominent white markings run from neck onto the side of the brown head. White-breasted. *Female*: A mottled brown color similar to other ducks, but can be recognized by slim appearance.

Range
Breeds primarily in northern United States and Canada west of the Great Lakes, and from Hudson Bay as far south as Iowa and northern California. Primarily a prairie nester, rarely found in wooded country; hence, the Pintail is not a common breeder in Minnesota. It is among the earliest of spring migrants and our waterfowl enthusiasts look for them in numbers prior to mid-April. Winters throughout southern states and as far south as Panama.

Principal breeding ranges of the Pintail in Minnesota and North America.

6

Pintail

♀

♂

♂

♀

GREEN-WINGED TEAL
(Anas crecca carolinensis)

Other Common Names
Sometimes mistakenly called Cinnamon Teal

Field Notes
Fast of flight, small in size and a real challenge to the hunter, the Green-wing is also recognized as a table delicacy. Mississippi Flyway data shows the Green-wing making up about 6 per cent of the duck harvest. This teal nests in dry locations near water, prefers a habitat of marshes and streams. Breeding in Minnesota is comparatively rare. Still, it has ranked among the "top four" of waterfowl harvested in Minnesota. Weight: Less than a pound; 12 ounces for females, 13 ounces average for males.

Field Marks
Appears "half-size" in proportion to other ducks. No large, light-colored patch on wings which mark the Blue-wing. *Male:* Small, gray, with brown head, conspicuous white mark on leading edge of wing. Shows iridescent green on head patch in sunlight. *Female:* Small, speckled duck with iridescent green speculum.

Range
Found over much of principal breeding grounds in northwestern quarter of United States, western half of Canada and in Alaska. Brood observations made in seven Minnesota counties, but migration observations show distribution throughout Minnesota. Migrates earlier than Blue-wing in spring and later in fall, although fall flight begins quite early. Winters primarily in southern states and Mexico.

Green-winged Teal

♀

♂

♂

BLUE-WINGED TEAL
(Anas discors)

Other Common Names
Teal, Blue-wing, Summer Teal

Field Notes
Fast, agile, colorful, sporty, tasty. The Blue-wing is all of these. He is a surface feeder, frequenting small, shallow ponds. No other duck can match his speed and agility. The Blue-wing rates high as a game bird, ranking second or third in the hunter's bag, particularly in the early part of the season. This tiny teal (males average 1 pound 2 ounces) is one of the last arrivals in the spring and among the first to head south come fall. The Blue-wing does not follow any "set rule" in nesting near water. Nests are often found up to a quarter-mile from water in grassy-type surroundings.

Field Marks
A "pint-sized" marsh duck with a large, light blue patch on the front of the wing can safely be called a Blue-wing. Although the Shoveller also has this light blue wing patch, the Shoveller is a larger duck, with a prominent bill. *Male*: Small, grayish-brown duck with chalky-blue patch on leading edge of wing, large white crescent in front of eye. *Female*: Mottled, with large blue patch on leading edge of wing.

Range
Breeding range extends from western New York to British Columbia and northern Nevada and includes all of Minnesota, where it is the most common breeding duck. This teal travels farther south than any other North American duck, ranging as far as the coast of Brazil and central Chile. Reaches peak numbers in Minnesota between September 8 and 15 and has usually departed by the third week in October.

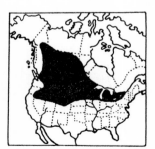

Principal breeding ranges of the Blue-winged Teal in Minnesota and North America.

10

Blue-winged Teal

♀   ♂   ♀   ♂

♂

CINNAMON TEAL AND SHOVELLER
(Anas cyanoptera cyanoptera) (Spatula clypeata)

Other Common Names
Shoveller: Spoonbill, Northern Shoveler
Cinnamon Teal: May be confused with Green-wing Teal

Field Notes
The Shoveller's large, shovel-like bill is the distinctive feature of this bird which makes up only a fraction of the Mississippi Flyway bag. But this resident of small prairie marshes is an interesting specimen for the waterfowl observer and hunter alike. That bill is especially adapted for surface feeding. The *Cinnamon Teal* is a close relative of the Blue-wing and, in breeding plumage, is a beautiful bird clad in cinnamon-red. Although this bird is not common in Minnesota, the species has been recorded in 13 counties.

Field Marks
The Shoveller is a small duck, but larger than teal, easily identified in all plumages by its spatulate bill. *Male*: Distinct black and white markings; belly and sides rufous-red; head dark and glossed with green; pale blue patch on leading edge of wing. Sits squat and low in water. *Female*: Mottled brown with blue patch on wing similar to male.

The *Cinnamon Teal* is quickly identified as a member of teal family by its small size. *Male*: Small, cinnamon-red with blue patches on leading edge of wing. *Female*: Mottled brown duck which also has blue wing-patches.

Range
The *Shoveller* is one of the most widely distributed ducks of the northern Hemisphere, ranging over northern North America and Eurasia from Great Britain eastward to northern Asia. *Cinnamon Teal* are also found in western North America, breeding primarily west of the Rocky Mountains and occasionally in the prairie states.

COMMON LOON
(Gavia Immer)

Other Common Names
Great Northern Diver

This large (5-9 lbs.) waterbird bears vague resemblance to a duck in silhouette, but the similarity ends there. Loons are larger and belong to an entirely different order of birds — Gaviformes. The Loon breeds in north country lakes which offer some seclusion. They are adept divers that live mainly on fish. Their populations have suffered because of pesticides transfer from fish on Lake Michigan. It is an attractive symbol of true wilderness with its echoing, weird call and water antics, one well worth preservation.

It is a fitting state bird for the land of 15,000 lakes — Minnesota.

12

Shoveller
♀
♂

Cinnamon Teal
♂   ♀

Cinnamon Teal
♂

Common Loon

GADWALL
(Anas strepera strepera)

Other Common Names
Gray Duck, Little Mallard

Field Notes
Although the Gadwall makes up only a small part of the game bag, his sporting quality is good and the meat generally acceptable. Even on the Central and Pacific Flyways, its favorite flight paths, it makes up less than three per cent of the total kill of ducks. It also travels the western edge of the Mississippi Flyway. Perhaps this fellow's most distinguishing feature is his lack of distinct features. Hence, the hunter often simply tags him as the "Gray Duck." The Gadwall is a medium sized bird, about 1 pound 10 ounces for males and 1 pound 9 ounces for females.

Field Marks
Look for a medium-sized duck with a slender body. Body coloration of the male is gray, but the hen is more brownish and quite similar to the hen Mallard and Pintail. The belly is whitish in both sexes. The male has a black rump. Note that both sexes of the Gadwall have white in the speculum, bordered by purplish-black. On the adult male there are patches of chestnut preceding the speculum.

Range
In North America, the main breeding range covers a generally rectangular area in northwestern United States and southwestern Canada, with only scattered breeding east of this range. Minnesota is on the eastern edge of the main breeding range. (Note: The Gadwall is found in fairly large numbers on Minnesota's Agassiz Refuge in Marshall County.) An interesting sidelight: There is a smaller subspecies of the Gadwall, thought to have originated from stranded birds, in the Fanning Islands of the southwest Pacific.

Principal breeding ranges of the Gadwall in Minnesota and North America.

14

Gadwall

♂ ♀
♂ ♂

EUROPEAN WIDGEON AND BALDPATE
(Mareca penelope) (Mareca americana)

Other Common Names

Baldpate: American Widgeon, Gray Duck, Widgeon, Bluebill

Field Notes

Here we have the *American and European versions of the Widgeon.* While similar in size and appearance, the *American Widgeon* nests over a large part of northern North America and the *European Widgeon*, while it has been recorded in a few Minnesota counties, is primarily a bird of Iceland, Europe and Asia. Our American Widgeon, commonly called the *Baldpate*, is a fine sporting bird, fast on the wing and easily decoyed. The Baldpate, while rating high as a sporting bird, makes up only a small part of the bag in Minnesota, and about 5 per cent of the waterfowl take on the Mississippi Flyway. Weight, about 1 pound 10 ounces for males; 1 pound 9 ounces for females.

Field Marks

The *European Widgeon's* head, bright cinnamon with buff cream crown, when too distant to show color, appears much darker than the rest of the bird, not unlike the appearance of the Baldpate. *American Widgeon or Baldpate*: The shining white crown of the male, which gives it is common name, is the best identifying feature. The Baldpate can also be recognized on the wing by the large white patch covering the front of the wing. *Male*: Brownish body with gray head and white crown; glossy green head patch; white patch on fore part of wing; blue bill with black tip. *Female*: Plainer and browner plumage and lacks white crown. Enough white on wing to serve as good field mark.

Range

The European Widgeon is an uncommon visitor in eastern North America. The Baldpate, or American Widgeon, breeds in western North America, east to Nebraska and Minnesota, and casually to western Pennsylvania. Generally found in ponds and bays.

Principal breeding ranges of the American Widgeon (Baldpate) in Minnesota and North America.

16

European Widgeon

♀
♂

American Baldpate

♂
♀

WOOD DUCK
(Aix sponsa)

Other Common Names
Summer Duck, Carolina Duck

Field Notes

The scientific name for the wood duck is *Aix Sponsa* which means (*Aix*-Greek) kind of waterfowl in Aristotle and (*Sponsa*-Latin) betrothed as in wedding dress, referring to its beautiful plumage. Thus the wood duck drake has come to be regarded as the sheik of waterfowl. He cannot be confused with any other species because the spectrum of color from his tail coverts to the tip of his bill are exclusive in design.

Woody is found in almost every state at some time or another and is as much at home in tree-tops (nipping off acorns) as in the small woodland pools he frequents. Woody's home is a natural tree cavity or old woodpecker hole and will often use man made nesting boxes.

The nest is usually several feet below the opening in the tree and is lined with down. When the young are ready to eject from the hole, mama woody whistles a signal and the young pop out like corks and "free fall" from considerable height. They are bouncy light fluffs of down that seemingly never get injured from their fall, and are ready to waddle behind mama duck to a nearby lake.

In the early 1900's the wood duck was nearly extinct but good management and protection from hunting made it remarkably plentiful to an estimated 2½ million population in 1965.

Weight, 1 pound 9 ounces for males, and 1 pound 2 ounces for females.

Field Marks

A bird known by its brilliant markings and habitat: woodland streams and forested bottomlands. In flight, the white belly contrasts sharply with dark breast and wings. Square tail, short neck and bill pointed downward also aid in-flight identification. *Male*: Strikingly handsome markings, most beautiful of North American waterfowl. Highly iridescent in good light. *Female*: A dark brown duck with white belly, dark crested head and distinct white patch surrounding eye.

Range

Found only in North America, the Wood Duck's breeding range is confined to the United States. One of Minnesota's most important nesting ducks and a bird which has prospered in woodland marshes all along the Mississippi flyway. Female wood ducks have even been recorded nesting atop hotels in downtown Minneapolis! Two widely separated populations: Eastern breeds from Nova Scotia to Lake Winnipeg and thence southward to coast of Texas; western population breeds from British Columbia south to San Joaquin Valley in California. Mississippi Flyway woodducks winter in Arkansas, Alabama, Mississippi, Louisiana.

18

Wood Duck

♂   ♀

CANVASBACK
(Aythya vallisneria)

Other Common Names
Can, White-back

Field Notes
The popular "Can" is a large diving duck and, in the fall, has a preference for certain lakes, such as famed Lake Christina in Minnesota's Grant and Douglas counties. The majestic fall flights of the Cans in years past thrilled thousands of hunters, but loss of habitat — and hunting pressure on this classic diver — has forced closing the season, or restricting harvest in several years, ranging as far back as 1936–37. In Minnesota, significant breeding numbers are found only in the northwest prairie pothole country. Big male Cans may top 3 pounds; females average 2 pounds 13 ounces. Decoys well, especially to large blocks of decoys.

Field Marks
Both male and female Canvasbacks can be distinguished by the long, sloping forehead and a bill which is almost as long as the head. *Male*: In breeding, plumage has an almost white back and wings; a dark head, neck and tail. Speculum of both sexes pearly gray, bill black, feet gray. *Female*: Grayish, with suggestion of red tones of male bird on neck and head. "Cans" may fly in lines or in V-formation.

Range
Breeds in Minnesota's northwest pothole country and occasionally in southern Wisconsin, but chiefly in the prairie region of north-central United States and central and western Canada. Winters from central New York southward, chiefly on salt or brackish bays to Gulf of Mexico.

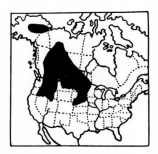

Principal breeding ranges of the Canvasback in Minnesota and North America.

20

Canvasback

♀

♂

♀

♂

♂

REDHEAD
(Aytha americana)

Other Common Names
American Porhard

Field Notes

In recent years, restrictions have been placed on the hunting of this diving duck, which normally makes up five per cent of the Flyway waterfowl harvest. Easily decoyed, eagerly sought by hunters, the Redhead also flies comparatively low, making it vulnerable. Its large size and superb flavor make it a favorite table bird. Somewhat similar in appearance to the larger Canvasback, this duck gets its name from the reddish-chestnut head and neck coloration. Average weight of the male Redhead is 2 pounds 8 ounces and of the female, 2 pounds 4 ounces.

Field Marks

The Redhead is primarily gray, while the Canvasback is very white. The Redhead's forehead is high in contrast to the Canvasback's low, sloping forehead. In flight, the Redhead appears short and chunky, as compared to the longer profile of the "Can." Redhead *males* have a round, red-brown head, along with coloration features outlined. *Female*: A brownish duck which has a broad gray wing and whitish patch near the base of the bill.

Range

The Redhead breeds in north-central United States and in southwestern and central Canada. Until the population decline in the late 1950's and early 1960's, it was a common breeder in non-wooded portions of Minnesota. Migrates rather late in spring and, in the fall, most Redheads have moved out of Minnesota by mid-November. Winters in southern United States along Atlantic and Gulf coasts and on the Pacific coast as far north as British Columbia.

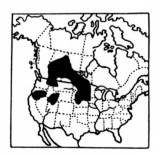

Principal breeding ranges of the Redhead in Minnesota and North America.

22

Redhead

♂

♀   ♀

♂

RING-NECKED DUCK
(Aythya collaris)

Other Common Names
Ringbill, Early Bluebill, Native Bluebill, Bluebill

Field Notes
Many insist he should be called Ring-bill, but Ring-neck he is, and one of our finest game birds at that. Sporty, tops on the table, the Ring-neck makes up a major portion of the Minnesota hunter's bag. In Minnesota, Ring-necks concentrate on such popular waters as Squaw Lake, Itasca County, and Big Rice Lake in Cass County. This duck commonly nests in forested areas and is usually found on boggy marshes or small lakes. Males average 1 pound 12 ounces and females 1 pound 8 ounces.

Field Marks
A medium sized duck, similar in size to the Lesser Scaup and sometimes mistaken for it; however, the Ring-neck has a gray speculum compared to the white speculum of the Lesser Scaup. *Male:* Head, chest and back are black, with prominent white mark in front of wing; bill crossed by two white rings. In flight, this is our only black-backed duck having a broad gray wing-stripe. *Female:* Brown, darkest on top of head and back, gray wing-stripe; ring on bill.

Range
Preference for wooded lake areas. Range extends from Newfoundland, New Brunswick, Quebec and Maine westward through Great Lakes area and west-central Canada. Ranks among top three of Minnesota's nesting ducks. Winters on both coasts and in states bordering Gulf of Mexico, but also winter-ranges in Mexico, Central America and Cuba.

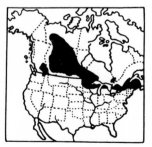

Principal breeding ranges of the Ring-necked Duck in Minnesota and North America.

Ring-necked Duck

♀

♂

♂

LESSER SCAUP
(Aythya affinis)

Other Common Names
Bluebill, Little Bluebill

Field Notes

The hunter affectionately calls him the Bluebill. And the Lesser Scaup is a great sporting bird for both pass and decoy shooting, making up almost 11 per cent of the bag in Minnesota. He may be seen in great "rafts" during early spring migrations and has two migrational populations: eastern and western. Eastern Scaup move from their breeding grounds southeasterly via the Central and Atlantic Flyways. Western birds, from Alberta and British Columbia, move southward through the western states. A hardy bird, the Lesser Scaup is one of the first to arrive come spring; among the last to leave in the fall.

Field Marks

The Lesser Scaup may be easily confused with the Greater Scaup. Differences are slight and confusing, even to the expert. The white on the wing of the Lesser Scaup is confined to the speculum, while on the Greater Scaup the white extends onto the primary feathers toward the wing tip. Head of the Lesser is also more angular and is glossed with dull purple (Greater has green-gloss). *Male Lesser:* Black on both ends and white in the middle. *Female:* Distinct white face mask behind bill.

Range

Canada's four western provinces comprise principal breeding range, along with the Yukon and western part of Northwest Territory. Two migrational populations, as indicated. Breeding in Minnesota confined to northwestern counties. Greatest concentrations of wintering Scaup are found on Gulf of Mexico; winter range also includes both coasts, Mexico, Central America and West Indies.

Principal breeding ranges of the Lesser Scaup in Minnesota and North America.

26

Lesser Scaup

♀ ♂ ♂ ♂ ♀

GREATER SCAUP
(Aythya marila mariloides)

Other Common Names
Bluebill, Big Bluebill, Northern Bluebill

Field Notes
Mississippi Flyway hunters take very few Greater Scaup because of their west-east fall migration pattern. Threre are no breeding records for the duck in Minnesota. Although few of this species are reported during migration periods, it is possible that the Greater Scaup may be a more frequent visitor, since this duck is easily confused with his cousin, the Lesser Scaup. The Greater Scaup weighs, on the average, 2 pounds, as compared to the average of 1 pound 14 ounce average for the Lesser Scaup.

Field Marks
The description for the Lesser Scaup applies to the Greater, except for variations in the white portion of the wing stripe and the greenish iridescence of the head feathers on the Greater, as compared to purplish sheen on the head of the Lesser. The Greater is slightly larger, but here again the difference is slight.

Range
Because there have been few leg band recoveries, migration patterns of the Greater Scaup from breeding grounds to the United States are obscure. Some birds are believed to move from western Alaska across the Pacific to the coast of Washington, while others fly on to the coast of California. Other Greater Scaup are believed to move from the Yukon and Northwest Territory southeastward across Canada to the Great Lakes and thence to the Atlantic seaboard.

Greater Scaup

♀

♂

RUDDY DUCK
(Oxyura jamaicensis rubida)

Other Common Names
Butterball

Field Notes
Nationally, and in the Upper Midwest, the Ruddy has no significant status as a game bird. But his antics on the more permanent marshes, his stiff, fan-like tail which he often holds erect, and the clown-like gyrations of this peppy rascal delight the observer. The conspicuous white cheeks on the Ruddy's head merely adds to the appeal of this chunky little duck. Rated among the "least terrestrial" of all ducks, the Ruddy is an expert diver and obtains much of its food by foraging the bottoms of streams and lakes. Average weight for males are 1 pound 6 ounces; females, 1 pound 2 ounces.

Field Marks
The fan-like tail of this small duck, which is often cocked vertically, the white cheek, and an unpatterned rusty-red coloration mark the *male* Ruddy in breeding plumage. He also wears a blackish cap and has a large, blue bill. The *female* is brownish-grey, with a dark cheek line. The male in winter is gray with white cheeks, and the bill is duller in color. The female's winter color is similar to the male, but she has a dark line crossing light cheeks.

Range
The Ruddy is the single North American representative of a widely distributed tribe of ducks known as "stiff tails," and close relatives of this species are found in such places as India, Turkey and Australia. The main breeding range of the Ruddy is Saskatchewan, Alberta, Manitoba and on the more stable marshes of the northern plains and western states. Winters chiefly along the coast of Florida and Gulf coast.

Interesting Characteristics. Ruddy female is completely silent and lays the largest egg of any duck. Male Ruddy has most striking courtship display of any species, being able to erect spiked tail and touch the back of his head with it. The Ruddy along with the Old Squaw is the only member of the duck tribes that has two distinct plumages one for summer and one for winter. The male also assists in rearing young, which other male species refrain from.

Principal breeding ranges of the Ruddy Duck in Minnesota and North America.

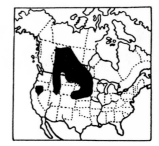

30

Ruddy Duck

♀   ♂

BUFFLEHEAD
(Bucephala albeola)

Other Common Names
Butterball

Field Notes
Although not significant as a game bird, the beautiful Bufflehead ranks high with those who treasure our waterfowl heritage. One of our smallest ducks, the Bufflehead is associated with woodland ponds and streams, as well as the parkland transition zones. Like the Wood Duck and the Goldeneye, this duck prefers tree cavities for nesting, and it may nest in a hole in a stream bank. Although much a part of the Minnesota scene during migration, the Bufflehead prefers more northerly nesting areas. Males average only a pound and females about 12 ounces.

Field Marks
One of our smallest ducks, the "Butterball" has a head which appears large in relation to body size. *Male*: Large white patch extending from eye to back of crown neck, underparts and sides white and wing is black, with a large white wing patch extending from leading edge to speculum. *Female*: A smaller, comparatively drab bird with an overall gray-brown coloration, white cheek spot and white wing-patch.

Range
Primary in the wooded regions of western Canada and eastern Alaska. Winters as far north as New England, British Columbia, along Atlantic, Pacific and Gulf coasts, in northern Mexico and in the United States where open water permits.

Bufflehead

♀

♂

♂

♀

♂

COMMON GOLDENEYE
(Bucephala clangula americana)

Other Common Names
American Goldeneye, Whistler

Field Notes

This handsome duck is the first to appear on our northern lakes and streams come spring and, although the Goldeneye makes up a minor part of the harvest, he is one of our finest ducks, providing sport late in the fall after many other ducks have migrated. A common characteristic: The Goldeneye nests in tree cavities. Nests have been found as high as 60 feet above the ground, and although shoreline trees are preferred, this duck will breed as far as a mile from water, and will readily accept nesting boxes. As more and more habitat is lost to agriculture, the northern wooded habitat becomes more vital in the management of the Goldeneye. Males average 2 pounds 2 ounces; females 1 pound 12 ounces.

Field Marks

The Goldeneye's flight is marked by a distinct "whistle" or singing sound, useful in identification and a characteristic which has given him the name "Whistler." *Males*: are white-looking, with a blackish, puffy, green-glossed head. Wings in flight show large white patches. Bright, golden-yellow eye with distinct white circle between bill and eye. *Female*: Plainly marked with brown head and grayish body.

Range

Breeding range is continent-wide in northern states and in Canada to the edge of the tundra. In mid-winter, may be seen on open water of Lake Superior or swift moving streams, and often in the vicinity of power plants. Also winters off the Atlantic and Pacific coasts.

Principal breeding ranges of the Common Goldeneye in Minnesota and North America.

34

Common Goldeneye

♂

♀

♀

BARROW'S GOLDENEYE
(Glaucionetta islandica)

Other Common Names
Whistler

Field Notes
Barrow's Goldeneye is a close relative of our Common or American Goldeneye. And it resembles our native duck in most respects. Although several sightings have been recorded in Minnesota, the observer should use caution in noting all characteristics before making positive identification. This bird has been seen on Lake of the Woods and observed in Minnesota's metropolitan area counties.

Field Marks
In contrast to our American Goldeneye, the Barrow's has a crescent-shaped patch between bill and eye and a greater amount of black on its sides. Further, the Barrow's head is glossed with purple instead of green and has a very different shape than the American version in that it has a more abrupt forehead and crown.

Range
The Barrow's Goldeneye nests in Iceland, Greenland, Labrador and also in North America from Alaska to northern Colorado. It winters from Labrador south along the Massachusetts' coast.

Barrow's Goldeneye

♂

♀

♂

OLD SQUAW
(Clangula hyemalis)

Other Common Names
Long-tailed Duck

Field Notes
The Old Squaw is a sea duck — and a resident of our Great Lakes. It has a preference for icy water and is a pleasure to observe on the vast reaches of Lake Superior. As a result, it is rarely recorded in the bag of upper midwest hunters. But "occasionals" do stray inland, as bag records indicate in Minnesota. This is a bird of two distinct plumages — summer and winter.

Field Marks
This is the only sea duck combining white on the body with unpatterned dark wings. The Old Squaw is a stocky, medium-sized, boldly pattern duck. *Male*: Summer plumage predominantly dark with white breast and belly. In winter, sharply patterned with dark brown and white. Elongate tail feathers at all seasons. *Female*: Lacks long, pointed tail feathers of the male and does not have as much dark plumage.

Range
Nests in the tundra and tundra forest of northern North America, Europe and Asia, as well as in Iceland and Greenland and many areas of the Arctic. Fairly common in Lake Superior off shorelines of Cook, Lake and St. Louis counties. Winters along Atlantic and Pacific coasts.

Interesting Characteristics. The Old Squaw is without peer as a diver among duck families. They have been caught in fishermen's gill nets on Lake Superior and other Great Lakes at depths of over 180 feet. As a result they have been accidentally destroyed as when single hauls of a net take as many as 1,500 birds.

The Old Squaw is also considered the songster of all ducks. Fur traders of the upper Yukon dubbed it the "organ duck" because of its melodious sounds. The Old Squaw's scientific name, *Clangula hyemalis* bears out it's vocal nature — meaning "noisy winter bird."

Old Squaw

♂ ♀

HARLEQUIN DUCK
(Histrionicus histrionicus)

Field Notes

The Harlequin is ranked with the Mandarin and Wood Duck in the "trio" of the world's most elegant ducks. It is a patchwork of color and spots which must be seen to be believed. It is also a rugged member of the waterfowl family, perfectly at home on roaring mountain streams, or on the rough, turbulent waters of the icy seas. This bird has been recorded several times in Minnesota, particularly along the north shore of Lake Superior, and there is a hint that it may nest in areas near Lake Superior, although no definite nesting observations have been made.

Field Marks

Bizarre coloration. *Male*: A rather small duck with a slate-blue head and body, elaborately marked with white, black and reddish-chestnut. Somewhat remindful of the Ruddy Duck in that it often cocks its tail. *Female*: A rather plain, dusky brown duck with three white spots, one behind the eye, one below it and one in front and above.

Range

There are two subspecies which are quite similar. This eastern subspecies breeds in Newfoundland, Labrador and Iceland, and winters on the Atlantic coast south to Long Island. Range of the western subspecies is from Alaska to central California.

Harlequin Duck

♀

♂

♂

RED-BREASTED MERGANSER
(Mergus serrator)

Other Common Names
Sawbill, Fish Duck

Field Notes
An interesting and beautiful duck, the Merganser is not an important game bird. A predominantly fish diet imparts a strong flavor to the Merganser's flesh. And a skilled fisherman he is, diving to feed on small fishes, crustaceans and, occasionally, on fish spawn. The Red-breasted Merganzer nests on the ground near water, generally among rocks and sometimes among the exposed roots of trees. This Merganser will average 2 pounds 10 ounces for males; 1 pound 13 ounces females.

Field Marks
Fairly large, with a long, red, cylindrical bill. The Red-breast may be distinguished from the American Merganser by its reddish-brown chest and white throat band. Both species have white wing patches. *Male*: Black head with green sheen and distinct crest; breast area at water-line is rusty, separated from head by wide, white band. Feet and bill red. *Female*: Similar to American Merganser, but female American Merganser has clear separation between reddish head and white throat, while female Red-Breast does not.

Range
Breeds in northern North America, Europe, Asia and Iceland. Nests from Minnesota eastward to Maine. May be seen in many parts of Minnesota during spring migration. While a few of these birds winter on the Great Lakes, the primary wintering ground is along the Pacific, Atlantic and Gulf coasts.

Red-Breasted Merganser

AMERICAN MERGANSER
(Mergus merganser americanus)

Other Common Names
Common Merganser, Big Fish Duck, Sawbill

Field Notes
The American Merganser is the largest of the three Merganser species found in Minnesota and the commonest cold-weather duck found on northern rivers. A "fishy taste" ranks this fellow quite low with the hunter, but his appearance rates him high with waterfowl enthusiasts who welcome the sight of his smart, formal attire during spring migrations. The American Merganser male will scale an average of 3 pounds 7 ounces; females 2 pounds 6 ounces. Like the Red-breasted, the American Merganser has a long, red bill with backward pointing teeth, is an excellent diver and feeds largely on small fishes.

Field Marks
The American Merganser is fond of flying "line formations" low over the water, following rivers and creeks. (Note the distinctions cited between the American and Red-breasted.) *Male*: A large duck with a long, white body, black back and a green-black head. "Whiteness" in flight and a rakish body are keys to identification. Bill and feet orange. In spring, breast is salmon colored. *Female*: Back gray, crested, brown head, large square white patch on wing.

Range
Nests along Minnesota's North Shore and parts of other northern states, and across the continent in Canada. Also in western mountain areas and south to northern New Mexico and central California. Winters along Pacific, Atlantic and Gulf coasts and inland from the Great Lakes southward.

American Merganser

♀

♂

♂

HOODED MERGANSER
(Lophodytes cucullatus)

Other Common Names
Fish Duck, Sawbill

Field Notes
Because they are relatively scarce, Hooded Mergansers are not particularly significant as a game bird. But they are much more palatable than their fellow Mergansers, and they are recognized as sporty waterfowl. Fond of our northern woodland streams and lakes, the Hooded Merganser nests in holes or cavities in trees and is the smallest of the three species of Mergansers found in Minnesota. It is an excellent diver and, like its fellow Mergansers, uses its serrated bill to capture fish.

Field Marks
Male in spring plumage is a handsome black and white bird with a fan-shaped white crest which it frequently spreads. The breast is white with two black bars in front of the wing. Sides are rufous brown. The *female* is mostly brown and has a crest of reddish-brown. There is a white wing patch. Differs from the other Mergansers in its smaller size and in that its teeth are vertical and not inclined backward.

Range
Breeds in suitable locations over most of the United States and southern Canada. In Minnesota, primary breeding range appears to be in the forested northeastern third of the state. Winters in southern United States, Mexico and along the Pacific and Atlantic coasts.

46

Hooded Merganser

♀

♂

♂

♀

WHITE-WINGED SCOTER
(Melanitta fusca deglandi)

COMMON EIDER
(Somateria mollissima)

Other Common Names
Scoter (Coot)

Field Notes

Scoters are large, black-hued ducks, commonly observed along coasts as they fly in low, wavering lines. The *White-wing* may be seen along Lake Superior and, at rare times, on some of Minnesota's large, inland lakes. It is easily identified by the white wing markings. Althought Eiders are the most oceanic of all ducks, the *Common Eider* may occasionally be seen on Lake Superior's waters. The Eider is a heavy, thick-necked bird which tends to fly low and sluggishly over the water, alternately flapping and sailing. Occasional specimens are taken by waterfowl hunters.

Field Marks

White-winged Scoter male: A large, heavy-set black bird with white wing-patches and a small patch just below the eye. *Female*: A dusky brown duck with white wing-patch. *Common Eider male*: The only duck with a black belly and white back. Breast and front part of wing white. The head is white with a black crown. *Female*: A large brown duck with a heavily barred body.

Range

The *White-winged Scoter* breeds across Canada from Alaska to the Gulf of St. Lawrence, and south to areas of central North Dakota. Winters to South Carolina, Great Lakes and along Gulf coast. The *Common Eider* nests in Maine, Greenland and Iceland on the Atlantic, and in the Aleutian Islands of the Pacific. Winters to Massachusetts and Long Island.

48

Common Eider **White-winged Scoter**

♀ ♂ ♂ ♀

SURF SCOTER
(Melanitta perspicillata)

Other Common Names
Skunk-head Coot

Field Notes
As one might expect, the Surf Scoter is rarely found in Minnesota's inland waters. It occurs most frequently on Lake Superior. The male is a velvety black for the most part, with one or two white patches on the crown of the head, markings which have inspired the nickname "Skunk-head Coot."

Field Marks
Like the other Scoters, the Surf Scoter is very dark in color. It is, however, somewhat smaller than the White-winged Scoter and does not have the white speculum of that species. *Male* has a white patch on forehead and large white patch on rear of head. *Female* is more brown than the other Scoters and has two whitish cheek patches.

Range
The Surf Scoter breeds in northwestern Canada and winters from Maine south to Florida, primarily in the coastal waters.

Surf Scoter

♀　　　　　♂

FULVOUS TREE DUCK
(Dendrocygna bicolor)

Other Common Names
Squealer

Field Notes
The nickname "Squealer" is prompted by this duck's squealing, double-noted whistle. Normally found in sub-tropical and tropical North America, this goose-like, long-legged and interesting species has been recorded a few times in Minnesota and along the northern portion of the Mississippi Flyway. It is also called the Fulvous Whistling Duck — sans trees — since it does not ordinarily frequent trees.

Field Marks
Waterfowl enthusiasts visiting Texas or Louisiana are most likely to observe this duck in the marshes and rice fields there. In addition to the characteristics mentioned, the Fulvous Tree Duck has a tawny body with a cream-colored stripe on the sides. Has slow wing-beats for a duck and, in flight, trails long legs behind the tail. Sexes similar in markings. Tall and gangly looking on land.

Range
Also found in Central and South America, Africa and Asia. In southern United States, range extends from south California eastward through parts of Arizona, Texas and Louisiana.

Fulvous Tree Duck

AMERICAN COOT
(*Fulica americana*)

Other Common Names
Mud Hen, Rice Hen

Field Notes
If the Coot were not so commonplace, if this bird had a more prestigious name, it would rank far higher in status among American waterfowl. *The Coot is not a duck.* It is related to rails and some of the shore birds. A bird of the marshes, seemingly adverse to flight unless pressed, the Coot is not held in esteem by hunters of the upper Mississippi Flyway. But in other sections of the Flyway, this bird is considered a table delicacy! The Coot has a chicken-like bill, webless feet and swims with its head moving in a pumping motion.

Field Marks
This is the only slate-colored, duck-like bird with a white bill. White patch under the tail; head and neck darker than the body. Legs and feet are green. Hind toe has a flap like that of diving ducks. When leaving water, feet skitter along surface for some distance. White border on trailing edge of wings is visible in flight.

Range
Breeds over much of North America and also in Cuba, Central America and Bahamas. Most common in agricultural areas of Flyway, although a few are found in wooded country. Winters along both coasts from Maine and Washington south, and across southern states, to Mexico, Central America and the West Indies.

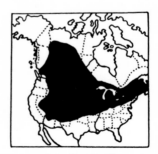

Principal breeding ranges of the Coot in Minnesota and North America.

American Coot

TOPOGRAPHY OF A DUCK

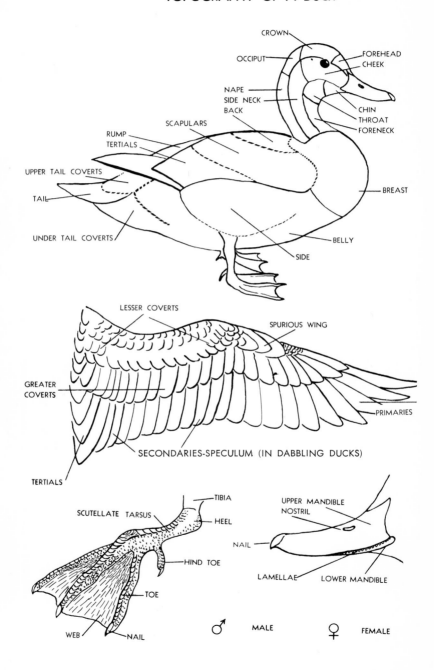

CROWN
OCCIPUT
FOREHEAD
CHEEK
NAPE
SIDE NECK
BACK
CHIN
THROAT
FORENECK
SCAPULARS
RUMP
TERTIALS
UPPER TAIL COVERTS
TAIL
UNDER TAIL COVERTS
BREAST
BELLY
SIDE

LESSER COVERTS
SPURIOUS WING
GREATER COVERTS
PRIMARIES
SECONDARIES-SPECULUM (IN DABBLING DUCKS)
TERTIALS

TIBIA
SCUTELLATE TARSUS
HEEL
HIND TOE
TOE
WEB
NAIL

UPPER MANDIBLE
NOSTRIL
NAIL
LAMELLAE
LOWER MANDIBLE

♂   MALE   ♀   FEMALE